THE GREAT LEARNING - THE DOCTRINE OF THE MEAN

CONFUCIUS   ZENGZI   ZISI

Translated by
JAMES LEGGE

CONTENTS

THE GREAT LEARNING

Chapter 1	3
Chapter 2	4

COMMENTARY OF THE PHILOSOPHER TSANG

Chapter 1	7
Chapter 2	8
Chapter 3	9
Chapter 4	10
Chapter 5	11
Chapter 6	12
Chapter 7	13
Chapter 8	14
Chapter 9	15
Chapter 10	17
Chapter 11	18
Chapter 12	19
Chapter 13	20
Chapter 14	21

THE DOCTRINE OF THE MEAN

Chapter 1	25
Chapter 2	26
Chapter 3	27
Chapter 4	28
Chapter 5	29
Chapter 6	30
Chapter 7	31
Chapter 8	32
Chapter 9	33
Chapter 10	34
Chapter 11	35
Chapter 12	36

Chapter 13	37
Chapter 14	38
Chapter 15	39
Chapter 16	40
Chapter 17	41
Chapter 18	42
Chapter 19	43
Chapter 20	44
Chapter 21	45
Chapter 22	47
Chapter 23	49
Chapter 24	50
Chapter 25	51
Chapter 26	52
Chapter 27	53
Chapter 28	54
Chapter 29	55
Chapter 30	56
Chapter 31	57
Chapter 32	58
Chapter 33	59
Chapter 34	60
Chapter 35	61
Chapter 36	62
Chapter 37	63
Chapter 38	64
Chapter 39	65

THE GREAT LEARNING

大學

Of uncertain authorship. Traditionally credited within China to Confucius's student Zengzi. Sometimes mistakenly credited to Confucius himself in western sources.

大學之道，在明明德，在親民，在止於至善。知止而后有定，定而后能靜，靜而后能安，安而后能慮，慮而后能得。物有本末，事有終始，知所先後，則近道矣。

What the Great Learning teaches, is to illustrate illustrious virtue; to renovate the people; and to rest in the highest excellence.

The point where to rest being known, the object of pursuit is then determined; and, that being determined, a calm unperturbedness may be attained to. To that calmness there will succeed a tranquil repose. In that repose there may be careful deliberation, and that deliberation will be followed by the attainment of the desired end.

Things have their root and their branches. Affairs have their end and their beginning. To know what is first and what is last will lead near to what is taught in the Great Learning.

古之欲明明德於天下者，先治其國；欲治其國者，先齊其家；欲齊其家者，先修其身；欲修其身者，先正其心；欲正其心者，先誠其意；欲誠其意者，先致其知，致知在格物。物格而後知至，知至而後意誠，意誠而後心正，心正而後身修，身修而後家齊，家齊而後國治，國治而後天下平。自天子以至於庶人，壹是皆以修身為本。其本亂而末治者否矣，其所厚者薄，而其所薄者厚，未之有也！此謂知本，此謂知之至也。

The ancients who wished to illustrate illustrious virtue throughout the kingdom, first ordered well their own states. Wishing to order well their states, they first regulated their families. Wishing to regulate their families, they first cultivated their persons. Wishing to cultivate their persons, they first rectified their hearts. Wishing to rectify their hearts, they first sought to be sincere in their thoughts. Wishing to be sincere in their thoughts, they first extended to the utmost their knowledge. Such extension of knowledge lay in the investigation of things.

Things being investigated, knowledge became complete. Their knowledge being complete, their thoughts were sincere. Their thoughts being sincere, their hearts were then rectified. Their hearts being rectified, their persons were cultivated. Their persons being cultivated, their families were regulated. Their families being regulated, their states were rightly governed. Their states being rightly governed, the whole kingdom was made tranquil and happy.

From the Son of Heaven down to the mass of the people, all must consider the cultivation of the person the root of everything besides.

It cannot be, when the root is neglected, that what should spring from it will be well ordered. It never has been the case that what was of great importance has been slightly cared for, and, at the same time, that what was of slight importance has been greatly cared for.

COMMENTARY OF THE PHILOSOPHER TSANG

《康誥》曰：「克明德。」《太甲》曰：「顧諟天之明命。」《帝典》曰：「克明峻德。」皆自明也。

In the Announcement to Kang, it is said, "He was able to make his virtue illustrious."

In the Tai Jia, it is said, "He contemplated and studied the illustrious decrees of Heaven."

In the Canon of the emperor (Yao), it is said, "He was able to make illustrious his lofty virtue."

These passages all show how those sovereigns made themselves illustrious.

湯之盤銘曰：「苟日新，日日新，又日新。」《康誥》曰：「作新民。」《詩》曰：「周雖舊邦，其命惟新。」是故君子無所不用其極。

On the bathing tub of Tang, the following words were engraved: "If you can one day renovate yourself, do so from day to day. Yea, let there be daily renovation."

In the Announcement to Kang, it is said, "To stir up the new people."

In the Book of Poetry, it is said, "Although Zhou was an ancient state the ordinance which lighted on it was new."

Therefore, the superior man in everything uses his utmost endeavors.

《詩》云：「邦畿千里，惟民所止。」《詩》云：「緡蠻黃鳥，止于丘隅。」子曰：「於止，知其所止，可以人而不如鳥乎？」《詩》云：「穆穆文王，於緝熙敬止！」為人君，止於仁；為人臣，止於敬；為人子，止於孝；為人父，止於慈；與國人交，止於信。

In the Book of Poetry, it is said, "The royal domain of a thousand li is where the people rest."

In the Book of Poetry, it is said, "The twittering yellow bird rests on a corner of the mound." The Master said, "When it rests, it knows where to rest. Is it possible that a man should not be equal to this bird?"

In the Book of Poetry, it is said, "Profound was King Wen. With how bright and unceasing a feeling of reverence did he regard his resting places!" As a sovereign, he rested in benevolence. As a minister, he rested in reverence. As a son, he rested in filial piety. As a father, he rested in kindness. In communication with his subjects, he rested in good faith.

《詩》云：「瞻彼淇澳，菉竹猗猗。有斐君子，如切如磋，如琢如磨。瑟兮僩兮，赫兮喧兮。有斐君子，終不可諠兮！」「如切如磋」者，道學也；「如琢如磨」者，自修也；「瑟兮僩兮」者，恂慄也；「赫兮喧兮」者，威儀也；「有斐君子，終不可諠兮」者，道盛德至善，民之不能忘也。《詩》云：「於戲前王不忘！」君子賢其賢而親其親，小人樂其樂而利其利，此以沒世不忘也。

In the Book of Poetry, it is said, "Look at that winding course of the Qi, with the green bamboos so luxuriant! Here is our elegant and accomplished prince! As we cut and then file; as we chisel and then grind: so has he cultivated himself. How grave is he and dignified! How majestic and distinguished! Our elegant and accomplished prince never can be forgotten." That expression-"As we cut and then file," the work of learning. "As we chisel and then grind," indicates that of self-culture. "How grave is he and dignified!" indicates the feeling of cautious reverence. "How commanding and distinguished! indicates an awe-inspiring deportment. "Our elegant and accomplished prince never can be forgotten," indicates how, when virtue is complete and excellence extreme, the people cannot forget them.

In the Book of Poetry, it is said, "Ah! the former kings are not forgotten." Future princes deem worthy what they deemed worthy, and love what they loved. The common people delight in what delighted them, and are benefited by their beneficial arrangements. It is on this account that the former kings, after they have quitted the world, are not forgotten.

子曰：「聽訟，吾猶人也，必也使無訟乎！」無情者不得盡其辭，大畏民志。此謂知本。

The Master said, "In hearing litigations, I am like any other body. What is necessary is to cause the people to have no litigations." So, those who are devoid of principle find it impossible to carry out their speeches, and a great awe would be struck into men's minds;-this is called knowing the root.

所謂誠其意者，毋自欺也，如惡惡臭，如好好色，此之謂自謙，故君子必慎其獨也！小人閒居為不善，無所不至，見君子而後厭然，掩其不善，而著其善。人之視己，如見其肺肝然，則何益矣！此謂誠於中，形於外，故君子必慎其獨也。曾子曰：「十目所視，十手所指，其嚴乎！」富潤屋，德潤身，心廣體胖，故君子必誠其意。

What is meant by "making the thoughts sincere." is the allowing no self-deception, as when we hate a bad smell, and as when we love what is beautiful. This is called self-enjoyment. Therefore, the superior man must be watchful over himself when he is alone.

There is no evil to which the mean man, dwelling retired, will not proceed, but when he sees a superior man, he instantly tries to disguise himself, concealing his evil, and displaying what is good. The other beholds him, as if he saw his heart and reins;-of what use is his disguise? This is an instance of the saying -"What truly is within will be manifested without." Therefore, the superior man must be watchful over himself when he is alone.

The disciple Zeng said, "What ten eyes behold, what ten hands point to, is to be regarded with reverence!"

Riches adorn a house, and virtue adorns the person. The mind is expanded, and the body is at ease. Therefore, the superior man must make his thoughts sincere.

所謂修身在正其心者：身有所忿懥，則不得其正；有所恐懼，則不得其正；有所好樂，則不得其正；有所憂患，則不得其正。心不在焉，視而不見，聽而不聞，食而不知其味。此謂修身在正其心。

What is meant by, "The cultivation of the person depends on rectifying the mind may be thus illustrated:-If a man be under the influence of passion he will be incorrect in his conduct. He will be the same, if he is under the influence of terror, or under the influence of fond regard, or under that of sorrow and distress.

When the mind is not present, we look and do not see; we hear and do not understand; we eat and do not know the taste of what we eat. This is what is meant by saying that the cultivation of the person depends on the rectifying of the mind.

所謂齊其家在修其身者：人之其所親愛而辟焉，之其所賤惡而辟焉，之其所畏敬而辟焉，之其所哀矜而辟焉，之其所敖惰而辟焉。故好而知其惡，惡而知其美者，天下鮮矣！故諺有之曰：「人莫知其子之惡，莫知其苗之碩。」此謂身不修不可以齊其家。

What is meant by "The regulation of one's family depends on the cultivation of his person is this:-men are partial where they feel affection and love; partial where they despise and dislike; partial where they stand in awe and reverence; partial where they feel sorrow and compassion; partial where they are arrogant and rude. Thus it is that there are few men in the world who love and at the same time know the bad qualities of the object of their love, or who hate and yet know the excellences of the object of their hatred.

Hence it is said, in the common adage,"A man does not know the wickedness of his son; he does not know the richness of his growing corn."

This is what is meant by saying that if the person be not cultivated, a man cannot regulate his family.

所謂治國必先齊其家者，其家不可教而能教人者，無之。故君子不出家而成教於國：孝者，所以事君也；弟者，所以事長也；慈者，所以使眾也。《康誥》曰：「如保赤子」，心誠求之，雖不中不遠矣。未有學養子而後嫁者也！一家仁，一國興仁；一家讓，一國興讓；一人貪戾，一國作亂。其機如此。此謂一言僨事，一人定國。堯、舜率天下以仁，而民從之；桀、紂率天下以暴，而民從之。其所令反其所好，而民不從。是故君子有諸己而後求諸人，無諸己而後非諸人。所藏乎身不恕，而能喻諸人者，未之有也。故治國在齊其家。《詩》云：「桃之夭夭，其葉蓁蓁；之子于歸，宜其家人。」宜其家人，而後可以教國人。《詩》云：「宜兄宜弟。」宜兄宜弟，而後可以教國人。《詩》云：「其儀不忒，正是四國。」其為父子兄弟足法，而後民法之也。此謂治國在齊其家。

What is meant by "In order rightly to govern the state, it is necessary first to regulate the family," is this: It is not possible for one to teach others, while he cannot teach his own family. Therefore, the ruler, without going beyond his family, completes the lessons for the state. There is filial piety - therewith the sovereign should be served. There is fraternal submission - therewith elders and superiors should be served. There is kindness - therewith the multitude should be treated.

In the Announcement to Kang, it is said, "Act as if you were watching over an infant." If a mother is really anxious about it, though she may not hit exactly the wants of her infant, she will not be far from doing so. There never has been a girl who learned to bring up a child, that she might afterwards marry.

From the loving example of one family a whole state becomes loving, and from its courtesies the whole state becomes courteous while, from the ambition and perverseness of the One man, the whole state may be led to rebellious disorder;-such is the nature of the influence. This verifies the saying, "Affairs may be ruined by a single sentence; a kingdom may be settled by its One man."

Yao and Shun led on the kingdom with benevolence and the people followed them. Chieh and Chau led on the kingdom with violence, and people followed them. The orders which these issued were contrary to the practices which they loved, and so the people did not follow them. On this account, the ruler must himself be possessed of the good qualities, and then he may require them in the people. He must not have the bad qualities in himself, and then he may require that they shall not be in the people. Never has there been a man, who, not having reference to his own character and wishes in dealing with others, was able effectually to instruct them.

Thus we see how the government of the state depends on the regulation of the family.

In the Book of Poetry, it is said, "That peach tree, so delicate and elegant!

How luxuriant is its foliage! This girl is going to her husband's house. She will rightly order her household." Let the household be rightly ordered, and then the people of the state may be taught.

In the Book of Poetry, it is said, "They can discharge their duties to their elder brothers. They can discharge their duties to their younger brothers." Let the ruler discharge his duties to his elder and younger brothers, and then he may teach the people of the state.

In the Book of Poetry, it is said, "In his deportment there is nothing wrong; he rectifies all the people of the state." Yes; when the ruler, as a father, a son, and a brother, is a model, then the people imitate him.

This is what is meant by saying, "The government of his kingdom depends on his regulation of the family."

所謂平天下在治其國者：上老老而民興孝，上長長而民興弟，上恤孤而民不倍，是以君子有絜矩之道也。所惡於上，毋以使下；所惡於下，毋以事上；所惡於前，毋以先後；所惡於後，毋以從前；所惡於右，毋以交於左；所惡於左，毋以交於右。此之謂絜矩之道。《詩》云：「樂只君子，民之父母。」民之所好好之，民之所惡惡之，此之謂民之父母。《詩》云：「節彼南山，維石巖巖。赫赫師尹，民具爾瞻。」有國者不可以不慎，辟則為天下戮矣。

What is meant by "The making the whole kingdom peaceful and happy depends on the government of his state," this: When the sovereign behaves to his aged, as the aged should be behaved to, the people become filial; when the sovereign behaves to his elders, as the elders should be behaved to, the people learn brotherly submission; when the sovereign treats compassionately the young and helpless, the people do the same. Thus the ruler has a principle with which, as with a measuring square, he may regulate his conduct.

What a man dislikes in his superiors, let him not display in the treatment of his inferiors; what he dislikes in inferiors, let him not display in the service of his superiors; what he hates in those who are before him, let him not therewith precede those who are behind him; what he hates in those who are behind him, let him not bestow on the left; what he hates to receive on the left, let him not bestow on the right:-this is what is called "The principle with which, as with a measuring square, to regulate one's conduct."

In the Book of Poetry, it is said, "How much to be rejoiced in are these princes, the parents of the people!" When a prince loves what the people love, and hates what the people hate, then is he what is called the parent of the people.

In the Book of Poetry, it is said, "Lofty is that southern hill, with its rugged masses of rocks! Greatly distinguished are you, O grand-teacher Yin, the people all look up to you. "Rulers of states may not neglect to be careful. If they deviate to a mean selfishness, they will be a disgrace in the kingdom.

《詩》云:「殷之未喪師,克配上帝。儀監于殷,峻命不易。」道得眾則得國,失眾則失國。是故君子先慎乎德。有德此有人,有人此有土,有土此有財,有財此有用。德者本也,財者末也,外本內末,爭民施奪。是故財聚則民散,財散則民聚。是故言悖而出者,亦悖而入;貨悖而入者,亦悖而出。《康誥》曰:「惟命不于常!」道善則得之,不善則失之矣。楚書曰:「楚國無以為寶,惟善以為寶。」舅犯曰:「亡人無以為寶,仁親以為寶。」

In the Book of Poetry, it is said, "Before the sovereigns of the Yin dynasty had lost the hearts of the people, they could appear before God. Take warning from the house of Yin. The great decree is not easily preserved." This shows that, by gaining the people, the kingdom is gained, and, by losing the people, the kingdom is lost.

On this account, the ruler will first take pains about his own virtue. Possessing virtue will give him the people. Possessing the people will give the territory. Possessing the territory will give him its wealth. Possessing the wealth, he will have resources for expenditure.

Virtue is the root; wealth is the result.

If he make the root his secondary object, and the result his primary, he will only wrangle with his people, and teach them rapine.

Hence, the accumulation of wealth is the way to scatter the people; and the letting it be scattered among them is the way to collect the people.

And hence, the ruler's words going forth contrary to right, will come back to him in the same way, and wealth, gotten by improper ways, will take its departure by the same.

In the Announcement to Kang, it is said, "The decree indeed may not always rest on us"; that is, goodness obtains the decree, and the want of goodness loses it.

In the Book of Chu, it is said, "The kingdom of Chu does not consider that to be valuable. It values, instead, its good men."

Duke Wen's uncle, Fan, said, "Our fugitive does not account that to be precious. What he considers precious is the affection due to his parent."

《秦誓》曰：「若有一个臣，斷斷兮無他技，其心休休焉，其如有容焉。人之有技，若己有之；人之彥聖，其心好之，不啻若自其口出。實能容之，以能保我子孫黎民，尚亦有利哉！人之有技，媢嫉以惡之；人之彥聖，而違之俾不通。實不能容，以不能保我子孫黎民，亦曰殆哉！」唯仁人放流之，迸諸四夷，不與同中國，此謂唯仁人為能愛人，能惡人。見賢而不能舉，舉而不能先，命也；見不善而不能退，退而不能遠，過也。好人之所惡，惡人之所好，是謂拂人之性，災必逮夫身。是故君子有大道，必忠信以得之，驕泰以失之。

In the Declaration of the Duke of Qin, it is said, "Let me have but one minister, plain and sincere, not pretending to other abilities, but with a simple, upright, mind; and possessed of generosity, regarding the talents of others as though he himself possessed them, and, where he finds accomplished and perspicacious men, loving them in his heart more than his mouth expresses, and really showing himself able to bear them and employ them:—such a minister will be able to preserve my sons and grandsons and black-haired people, and benefits likewise to the kingdom may well be looked for from him. But if it be his character, when he finds men of ability, to be jealous and hate them; and, when he finds accomplished and perspicacious men, to oppose them and not allow their advancement, showing himself really not able to bear them: such a minister will not be able to protect my sons and grandsons and people; and may he not also be pronounced dangerous to the state?"

It is only the truly virtuous man who can send away such a man and banish him, driving him out among the barbarous tribes around, determined not to dwell along with him in the Middle Kingdom. This is in accordance with the saying, "It is only the truly virtuous man who can love or who can hate others."

To see men of worth and not be able to raise them to office; to raise them to office, but not to do so quickly:—this is disrespectful. To see bad men and not be able to remove them; to remove them, but not to do so to a distance:—this is weakness.

To love those whom men hate, and to hate those whom men love;—this is to outrage the natural feeling of men. Calamities cannot fail to come down on him who does so. Thus we see that the sovereign has a great course to pursue. He must show entire self-devotion and sincerity to attain it, and by pride and extravagance he will fail of it.

生財有大道。生之者眾，食之者寡，為之者疾，用之者舒，則財恒足矣。仁者以財發身，不仁者以身發財。未有上好仁而下不好義者也，未有好義其事不終者也，未有府庫財非其財者也。

There is a great course also for the production of wealth. Let the producers be many and the consumers few. Let there be activity in the production, and economy in the expenditure. Then the wealth will always be sufficient.

The virtuous ruler, by means of his wealth, makes himself more distinguished. The vicious ruler accumulates wealth, at the expense of his life.

Never has there been a case of the sovereign loving benevolence, and the people not loving righteousness. Never has there been a case where the people have loved righteousness, and the affairs of the sovereign have not been carried to completion. And never has there been a case where the wealth in such a state, collected in the treasuries and arsenals, did not continue in the sovereign's possession.

孟獻子曰：「畜馬乘，不察於雞豚；伐冰之家，不畜牛羊；百乘之家，不畜聚斂之臣。與其有聚斂之臣，寧有盜臣。」此謂國不以利為利，以義為利也。長國家而務財用者，必自小人矣。彼為善之，小人之使為國家，災害并至。雖有善者，亦無如之何矣！此謂國不以利為利，以義為利也。

The officer Meng Xian said, "He who keeps horses and a carriage does not look after fowls and pigs. The family which keeps its stores of ice does not rear cattle or sheep. So, the house which possesses a hundred chariots should not keep a minister to look out for imposts that he may lay them on the people. Than to have such a minister, it were better for that house to have one who should rob it of its revenues." This is in accordance with the saying:-"In a state, pecuniary gain is not to be considered to be prosperity, but its prosperity will be found in righteousness."

When he who presides over a state or a family makes his revenues his chief business, he must be under the influence of some small, mean man. He may consider this man to be good; but when such a person is employed in the administration of a state or family, calamities from Heaven, and injuries from men, will befall it together, and, though a good man may take his place, he will not be able to remedy the evil. This illustrates again the saying, "In a state, gain is not to be considered prosperity, but its prosperity will be found in righteousness."

THE DOCTRINE OF THE MEAN

中庸

The *Doctrine of the Mean* is both a doctrine of Confucianism and also the title of one of the Four Books of Confucian philosophy. The text is attributed to Zisi, the only grandson of Confucius.

天命之謂性，率性之謂道，修道之謂教。道也者，不可須臾離也，可離非道也。是故君子戒慎乎其所不睹，恐懼乎其所不聞。莫見乎隱，莫顯乎微。故君子慎其獨也。喜怒哀樂之未發，謂之中；發而皆中節，謂之和；中也者，天下之大本也；和也者，天下之達道也。致中和，天地位焉，萬物育焉。

What Heaven has conferred is called The Nature; an accordance with this nature is called The Path of duty; the regulation of this path is called Instruction. The path may not be left for an instant. If it could be left, it would not be the path. On this account, the superior man does not wait till he sees things, to be cautious, nor till he hears things, to be apprehensive. There is nothing more visible than what is secret, and nothing more manifest than what is minute. Therefore the superior man is watchful over himself, when he is alone. While there are no stirrings of pleasure, anger, sorrow, or joy, the mind may be said to be in the state of Equilibrium. When those feelings have been stirred, and they act in their due degree, there ensues what may be called the state of Harmony. This Equilibrium is the great root from which grow all the human actings in the world, and this Harmony is the universal path which they all should pursue. Let the states of equilibrium and harmony exist in perfection, and a happy order will prevail throughout heaven and earth, and all things will be nourished and flourish.

仲尼曰：「君子中庸，小人反中庸。君子之中庸也，君子而時中；小人之中庸也，小人而無忌憚也。」

Zhong-ni said, "The superior man embodies the course of the Mean; the mean man acts contrary to the course of the Mean. The superior man's embodying the course of the Mean is because he is a superior man, and so always maintains the Mean. The mean man's acting contrary to the course of the Mean is because he is a mean man, and has no caution."

子曰：「中庸其至矣乎！民鮮能久矣！」

The Master said, "Perfect is the virtue which is according to the Mean! Rare have they long been among the people, who could practice it!"

子曰：「道之不行也，我知之矣：知者過之，愚者不及也。道之不明也，我知之矣：賢者過之，不肖者不及也。人莫不飲食也，鮮能知味也。」

The Master said, "I know how it is that the path of the Mean is not walked in: The knowing go beyond it, and the stupid do not come up to it. I know how it is that the path of the Mean is not understood: The men of talents and virtue go beyond it, and the worthless do not come up to it. There is no body but eats and drinks. But they are few who can distinguish flavors."

子曰：「道其不行矣夫。」

The Master said, "Alas! How is the path of the Mean untrodden!"

子曰：「舜其大知也與！舜好問而好察邇言，隱惡而揚善，執其兩端，用其中於民，其斯以為舜乎！」

The Master said, "There was Shun: He indeed was greatly wise! Shun loved to question others, and to study their words, though they might be shallow. He concealed what was bad in them and displayed what was good. He took hold of their two extremes, determined the Mean, and employed it in his government of the people. It was by this that he was Shun!"

子曰：「人皆曰『予知』，驅而納諸罟擭陷阱之中，而莫之知辟也。人皆曰『予知』，擇乎中庸，而不能期月守也。」

The Master said "Men all say, 'We are wise'; but being driven forward and taken in a net, a trap, or a pitfall, they know not how to escape. Men all say, 'We are wise'; but happening to choose the course of the Mean, they are not able to keep it for a round month."

子曰：「回之為人也，擇乎中庸，得一善，則拳拳服膺而弗失之矣。」

The Master said "This was the manner of Hui: he made choice of the Mean, and whenever he got hold of what was good, he clasped it firmly, as if wearing it on his breast, and did not lose it."

子曰：「天下國家可均也，爵祿可辭也，白刃可蹈也，中庸不可能也。」

The Master said, "The kingdom, its states, and its families, may be perfectly ruled; dignities and emoluments may be declined; naked weapons may be trampled under the feet; but the course of the Mean cannot be attained to."

子路問強。子曰：「南方之強與？北方之強與？抑而強與？寬柔以教，不報無道，南方之強也，君子居之。衽金革，死而不厭，北方之強也，而強者居之。故君子和而不流，強哉矯！中立而不倚，強哉矯！國有道，不變塞焉，強哉矯！國無道，至死不變，強哉矯！」

Zi-lu asked about energy. The Master said, "Do you mean the energy of the South, the energy of the North, or the energy which you should cultivate yourself? To show forbearance and gentleness in teaching others; and not to revenge unreasonable conduct - this is the energy of southern regions, and the good man makes it his study. To lie under arms; and meet death without regret - this is the energy of northern regions, and the forceful make it their study. Therefore, the superior man cultivates a friendly harmony, without being weak. How firm is he in his energy! He stands erect in the middle, without inclining to either side. How firm is he in his energy! When good principles prevail in the government of his country, he does not change from what he was in retirement. How firm is he in his energy! When bad principles prevail in the country, he maintains his course to death without changing. How firm is he in his energy!"

子曰：「素隱行怪，後世有述焉，吾弗為之矣。君子遵道而行，半途而廢，吾弗能已矣。君子依乎中庸，遁世不見知而不悔，唯聖者能之。

The Master said, "To live in obscurity, and yet practice wonders, in order to be mentioned with honor in future ages:-this is what I do not do. The good man tries to proceed according to the right path, but when he has gone halfway, he abandons it:-I am not able so to stop. The superior man accords with the course of the Mean. Though he may be all unknown, unregarded by the world, he feels no regret. It is only the sage who is able for this.

君子之道費而隱。夫婦之愚，可以與知焉，及其至也，雖聖人亦有所不知焉；夫婦之不肖，可以能行焉，及其至也，雖聖人亦有所不能焉。天地之大也，人猶有所憾，故君子語大，天下莫能載焉；語小，天下莫能破焉。《詩》云：『鳶飛戾天，魚躍于淵。』言其上下察也。君子之道，造端乎夫婦，及其至也，察乎天地。」

The way which the superior man pursues, reaches wide and far, and yet is secret. Common men and women, however ignorant, may intermeddle with the knowledge of it; yet in its utmost reaches, there is that which even the sage does not know. Common men and women, however much below the ordinary standard of character, can carry it into practice; yet in its utmost reaches, there is that which even the sage is not able to carry into practice. Great as heaven and earth are, men still find some things in them with which to be dissatisfied. Thus it is that, were the superior man to speak of his way in all its greatness, nothing in the world would be found able to embrace it, and were he to speak of it in its minuteness, nothing in the world would be found able to split it. It is said in the Book of Poetry, "The hawk flies up to heaven; the fishes leap in the deep." This expresses how this way is seen above and below. The way of the superior man may be found, in its simple elements, in the intercourse of common men and women; but in its utmost reaches, it shines brightly through heaven and earth.

子曰：「道不遠人。人之為道而遠人，不可以為道。《詩》云：『伐柯伐柯，其則不遠。』執柯以伐柯，睨而視之，猶以為遠。故君子以人治人，改而止。忠恕違道不遠，施諸己而不願，亦勿施於人。君子之道四，丘未能一焉：所求乎子以事父，未能也；所求乎臣以事君，未能也；所求乎弟以事兄，未能也；所求乎朋友先施之，未能也。庸德之行，庸言之謹，有所不足，不敢不勉，有餘不敢盡；言顧行，行顧言，君子胡不慥慥爾！

The Master said "The path is not far from man. When men try to pursue a course, which is far from the common indications of consciousness, this course cannot be considered The Path. In the Book of Poetry, it is said, 'In hewing an ax handle, in hewing an ax handle, the pattern is not far off. We grasp one ax handle to hew the other; and yet, if we look askance from the one to the other, we may consider them as apart. Therefore, the superior man governs men, according to their nature, with what is proper to them, and as soon as they change what is wrong, he stops. When one cultivates to the utmost the principles of his nature, and exercises them on the principle of reciprocity, he is not far from the path. What you do not like when done to yourself, do not do to others. In the way of the superior man there are four things, to not one of which have I as yet attained.-To serve my father, as I would require my son to serve me: to this I have not attained; to serve my prince as I would require my minister to serve me: to this I have not attained; to serve my elder brother as I would require my younger brother to serve me: to this I have not attained; to set the example in behaving to a friend, as I would require him to behave to me: to this I have not attained. Earnest in practicing the ordinary virtues, and careful in speaking about them, if, in his practice, he has anything defective, the superior man dares not but exert himself; and if, in his words, he has any excess, he dares not allow himself such license. Thus his words have respect to his actions, and his actions have respect to his words; is it not just an entire sincerity which marks the superior man?

君子素其位而行，不願乎其外。素富貴，行乎富貴；素貧賤，行乎貧賤；素夷狄，行乎夷狄；素患難，行乎患難：君子無入而不自得焉。在上位不陵下，在下位不援上，正己而不求於人，則無怨。上不怨天，下不尤人。故君子居易以俟命，小人行險以徼幸。」

The superior man does what is proper to the station in which he is; he does not desire to go beyond this. In a position of wealth and honor, he does what is proper to a position of wealth and honor. In a poor and low position, he does what is proper to a poor and low position. Situated among barbarous tribes, he does what is proper to a situation among barbarous tribes. In a position of sorrow and difficulty, he does what is proper to a position of sorrow and difficulty. The superior man can find himself in no situation in which he is not himself. In a high situation, he does not treat with contempt his inferiors. In a low situation, he does not court the favor of his superiors. He rectifies himself, and seeks for nothing from others, so that he has no dissatisfactions. He does not murmur against Heaven, nor grumble against men. Thus it is that the superior man is quiet and calm, waiting for the appointments of Heaven, while the mean man walks in dangerous paths, looking for lucky occurrences.

子曰：「射有似乎君子，失諸正鵠，反求諸其身。君子之道，辟如行遠必自邇，辟如登高必自卑。《詩》曰：『妻子好合，如鼓瑟琴；兄弟既翕，和樂且耽。宜爾室家，樂爾妻帑。』」子曰：「父母其順矣乎！」

The Master said, "In archery we have something like the way of the superior man. When the archer misses the center of the target, he turns round and seeks for the cause of his failure in himself. The way of the superior man may be compared to what takes place in traveling, when to go to a distance we must first traverse the space that is near, and in ascending a height, when we must begin from the lower ground. It is said in the Book of Poetry, "Happy union with wife and children is like the music of lutes and harps. When there is concord among brethren, the harmony is delightful and enduring. Thus may you regulate your family, and enjoy the pleasure of your wife and children." The Master said, "In such a state of things, parents have entire complacence!"

子曰：「鬼神之為德，其盛矣乎！視之而弗見，聽之而弗聞，體物而不可遺。使天下之人齊明盛服，以承祭祀，洋洋乎如在其上，如在其左右。《詩》曰：『神之格思，不可度思！矧可射思！』夫微之顯，誠之不可掩如此夫。」

The Master said, "How abundantly do spiritual beings display the powers that belong to them! We look for them, but do not see them; we listen to, but do not hear them; yet they enter into all things, and there is nothing without them. They cause all the people in the kingdom to fast and purify themselves, and array themselves in their richest dresses, in order to attend at their sacrifices. Then, like overflowing water, they seem to be over the heads, and on the right and left of their worshippers. It is said in the Book of Poetry, 'The approaches of the spirits, you cannot surmise; and can you treat them with indifference?' Such is the manifestness of what is minute! Such is the impossibility of repressing the outgoings of sincerity!"

子曰：「舜其大孝也與！德為聖人，尊為天子，富有四海之內。宗廟饗之，子孫保之。故大德必得其位，必得其祿，必得其名，必得其壽。故天之生物，必因其材而篤焉。故栽者培之，傾者覆之。《詩》曰：『嘉樂君子，憲憲令德！宜民宜人，受祿于天。保佑命之，自天申之！』故大德者必受命。」

The Master said, "How greatly filial was Shun! His virtue was that of a sage; his dignity was the throne; his riches were all within the four seas. He offered his sacrifices in his ancestral temple, and his descendants preserved the sacrifices to himself. Therefore having such great virtue, it could not but be that he should obtain the throne, that he should obtain those riches, that he should obtain his fame, that he should attain to his long life. Thus it is that Heaven, in the production of things, is sure to be bountiful to them, according to their qualities. Hence the tree that is flourishing, it nourishes, while that which is ready to fall, it overthrows. In the Book of Poetry, it is said, 'The admirable amiable prince displayed conspicuously his excelling virtue, adjusting his people, and adjusting his officers. Therefore, he received from Heaven his emoluments of dignity. It protected him, assisted him, decreed him the throne; sending from Heaven these favors, as it were repeatedly.' We may say therefore that he who is greatly virtuous will be sure to receive the appointment of Heaven."

子曰：「無憂者其惟文王乎！以王季為父，以武王為子，父作之，子述之。武王纘大王、王季、文王之緒，壹戎衣而有天下，身不失天下之顯名；尊為天子，富有四海之內。宗廟饗之，子孫保之。武王末受命，周公成文、武之德，追王大王、王季，上祀先公以天子之禮。斯禮也，達乎諸侯、大夫及士、庶人。父為大夫，子為士，葬以大夫，祭以士。父為士，子為大夫，葬以士，祭以大夫。期之喪，達乎大夫；三年之喪，達乎天子；父母之喪，無貴賤，一也。」

The Master said, "It is only King Wen of whom it can be said that he had no cause for grief! His father was King Ji, and his son was King Wu. His father laid the foundations of his dignity, and his son transmitted it. King Wu continued the enterprise of King Tai, King Ji, and King Wen. He once buckled on his armor, and got possession of the kingdom. He did not lose the distinguished personal reputation which he had throughout the kingdom. His dignity was the royal throne. His riches were the possession of all within the four seas. He offered his sacrifices in his ancestral temple, and his descendants maintained the sacrifices to himself. It was in his old age that King Wu received the appointment to the throne, and the duke of Zhou completed the virtuous course of Wen and Wu. He carried up the title of king to Tai and Ji, and sacrificed to all the former dukes above them with the royal ceremonies. And this rule he extended to the princes of the kingdom, the great officers, the scholars, and the common people. If the father were a great officer and the son a scholar, then the burial was that due to a great officer, and the sacrifice that due to a scholar. If the father were a scholar and the son a great officer, then the burial was that due to a scholar, and the sacrifice that due to a great officer. The one year's mourning was made to extend only to the great officers, but the three years' mourning extended to the Son of Heaven. In the mourning for a father or mother, he allowed no difference between the noble and the mean.

子曰：「武王、周公，其達孝矣乎！夫孝者：善繼人之志，善述人之事者也。春、秋修其祖廟，陳其宗器，設其裳衣，薦其時食。宗廟之禮，所以序昭穆也；序爵，所以辨貴賤也；序事，所以辨賢也；旅酬下為上，所以逮賤也；燕毛，所以序齒也。踐其位，行其禮，奏其樂，敬其所尊，愛其所親，事死如事生，事亡如事存，孝之至也。郊社之禮，所以事上帝也；宗廟之禮，所以祀乎其先也。明乎郊社之禮、禘嘗之義，治國其如示諸掌乎！」

The Master said, "How far-extending was the filial piety of King Wu and the duke of Zhou! Now filial piety is seen in the skillful carrying out of the wishes of our forefathers, and the skillful carrying forward of their undertakings. In spring and autumn, they repaired and beautified the temple halls of their fathers, set forth their ancestral vessels, displayed their various robes, and presented the offerings of the several seasons. By means of the ceremonies of the ancestral temple, they distinguished the royal kindred according to their order of descent. By ordering the parties present according to their rank, they distinguished the more noble and the less. By the arrangement of the services, they made a distinction of talents and worth. In the ceremony of general pledging, the inferiors presented the cup to their superiors, and thus something was given the lowest to do. At the concluding feast, places were given according to the hair, and thus was made the distinction of years. They occupied the places of their forefathers, practiced their ceremonies, and performed their music. They reverenced those whom they honored, and loved those whom they regarded with affection. Thus they served the dead as they would have served them alive; they served the departed as they would have served them had they been continued among them - the height of filial piety. By the ceremonies of the sacrifices to Heaven and Earth they served God, and by the ceremonies of the ancestral temple they sacrificed to their ancestors. He who understands the ceremonies of the sacrifices to Heaven and Earth, and the meaning of the several sacrifices to ancestors, would find the government of a kingdom as easy as to look into his palm!"

哀公問政。子曰：「文、武之政，布在方策，其人存，則其政舉；其人亡，則其政息。人道敏政，地道敏樹。夫政也者，蒲盧也。故為政在人，取人以身，修身以道，修道以仁。仁者人也，親親為大；義者宜也，尊賢為大。親親之殺，尊賢之等，禮所生也。在下位不獲乎上，民不可得而治矣！故君子不可以不修身；思修身，不可以不事親；思事親，不可以不知人；思知人，不可以不知天。天下之達道五，所以行之者三，曰：君臣也，父子也，夫婦也，昆弟也，朋友之交也，五者天下之達道也。知仁勇三者，天下之達德也，所以行之者一也。或生而知之，或學而知之，或困而知之，及其知之，一也；或安而行之，或利而行之，或勉強而行之，及其成功，一也。」

The Duke Ai asked about government. The Master said, "The government of Wen and Wu is displayed in the records - the tablets of wood and bamboo. Let there be the men and the government will flourish; but without the men, their government decays and ceases. With the right men the growth of government is rapid, just as vegetation is rapid in the earth; and, moreover, their government might be called an easily-growing rush. Therefore the administration of government lies in getting proper men. Such men are to be got by means of the ruler's own character. That character is to be cultivated by his treading in the ways of duty. And the treading those ways of duty is to be cultivated by the cherishing of benevolence. Benevolence is the characteristic element of humanity, and the great exercise of it is in loving relatives. Righteousness is the accordance of actions with what is right, and the great exercise of it is in honoring the worthy. The decreasing measures of the love due to relatives, and the steps in the honor due to the worthy, are produced by the principle of propriety. When those in inferior situations do not possess the confidence of their superiors, they cannot retain the government of the people. Hence the sovereign may not neglect the cultivation of his own character. Wishing to cultivate his character, he may not neglect to serve his parents. In order to serve his parents, he may not neglect to acquire knowledge of men. In order to know men, he may not dispense with a knowledge of Heaven. The duties of universal obligation are five and the virtues wherewith they are practiced are three. The duties are those between sovereign and minister, between father and son, between husband and wife, between elder brother and younger, and those belonging to the intercourse of friends. Those five are the duties of universal obligation. Knowledge, magnanimity, and energy, these three, are the virtues universally binding. And the means by which they carry the duties into practice is singleness. Some are born with the knowledge of those duties; some know them by study; and some acquire the knowledge after a painful feeling of their ignorance. But the knowledge being possessed, it comes to the same thing. Some practice them with a natural ease; some from a desire for their advantages; and some by strenuous effort. But the achievement being made, it comes to the same thing."

子曰：「好學近乎知，力行近乎仁，知恥近乎勇。知斯三者，則知所以修身；知所以修身，則知所以治人；知所以治人，則知所以治天下國家矣。凡為天下國家有九經，曰：修身也，尊賢也，親親也，敬大臣也，體群臣也，子庶民也，來百工也，柔遠人也，懷諸侯也。修身則道立，尊賢則不惑，親親則諸父昆弟不怨，敬大臣則不眩，體群臣則士之報禮重，子庶民則百姓勸，來百工則財用足，柔遠人則四方歸之，懷諸侯則天下畏之。齊明盛服，非禮不動，所以修身也；去讒遠色，賤貨而貴德，所以勸賢也；尊其位，重其祿，同其好惡，所以勸親親也；官盛任使，所以勸大臣也；忠信重祿，所以勸士也；時使薄斂，所以勸百姓也；日省月試，既廩稱事，所以勸百工也；送往迎來，嘉善而矜不能，所以柔遠人也；繼絕世，舉廢國，治亂持危，朝聘以時，厚往而薄來，所以懷諸侯也。凡為天下國家有九經，所以行之者一也。」

The Master said, "To be fond of learning is to be near to knowledge. To practice with vigor is to be near to magnanimity. To possess the feeling of shame is to be near to energy. He who knows these three things knows how to cultivate his own character. Knowing how to cultivate his own character, he knows how to govern other men. Knowing how to govern other men, he knows how to govern the kingdom with all its states and families. All who have the government of the kingdom with its states and families have nine standard rules to follow;-viz., the cultivation of their own characters; the honoring of men of virtue and talents; affection towards their relatives; respect towards the great ministers; kind and considerate treatment of the whole body of officers; dealing with the mass of the people as children; encouraging the resort of all classes of artisans; indulgent treatment of men from a distance; and the kindly cherishing of the princes of the states. By the ruler's cultivation of his own character, the duties of universal obligation are set forth. By honoring men of virtue and talents, he is preserved from errors of judgment. By showing affection to his relatives, there is no grumbling nor resentment among his uncles and brethren. By respecting the great ministers, he is kept from errors in the practice of government. By kind and considerate treatment of the whole body of officers, they are led to make the most grateful return for his courtesies. By dealing with the mass of the people as his children, they are led to exhort one another to what is good. By encouraging the resort of an classes of artisans, his resources for expenditure are rendered ample. By indulgent treatment of men from a distance, they are brought to resort to him from all quarters. And by kindly cherishing the princes of the states, the whole kingdom is brought to revere him. Self-adjustment and purification, with careful regulation of his dress, and the not making a movement contrary to the rules of propriety this is the way for a ruler to cultivate his person. Discarding slanderers, and keeping himself from the seductions of beauty; making light of riches, and giving honor to virtue-this is the way for him to encourage men of worth and talents. Giving them places of honor and large emolument. and sharing with them in their likes and dislikes-this is the way for him to encourage his relatives to love him. Giving them numerous officers to discharge their orders and commissions:-this is the way for him to encourage the great ministers. According to them a generous confidence, and making their emoluments large:-this is the way to encourage the body of officers. Employing them only at the proper times, and making the imposts light:-this is the way to encourage the people. By daily examinations and monthly trials, and by making their rations in accordance with their labors:-this is the way to encourage the classes of artisans. To escort them on their departure and meet them on their coming; to commend the good among them, and show compassion to the incompetent:-this is the way to treat indulgently men from a distance. To restore families whose line of succession has been broken, and to revive states that have been extinguished; to reduce to order states that are in confusion, and support those which are in peril; to have fixed times for their own reception at court, and the reception of their envoys; to send them away after liberal treatment, and welcome their coming with small contributions: this is the way to cherish the princes of the states. All who have the government of the kingdom with its states and families have the above nine standard rules. And the means by which they are carried into practice is singleness.

「凡事豫則立，不豫則廢。言前定則不跲，事前定則不困，行前定則不疚，道前定則不窮。在下位不獲乎上，民不可得而治矣；獲乎上有道：不信乎朋友，不獲乎上矣；信乎朋友有道：不順乎親，不信乎朋友矣；順乎親有道：反諸身不誠，不順乎親矣；誠身有道：不明乎善，不誠乎身矣。誠者，天之道也；誠之者，人之道也。誠者不勉而中，不思而得，從容中道，聖人也。誠之者，擇善而固執之者也。博學之，審問之，慎思之，明辨之，篤行之。有弗學，學之弗能，弗措也；有弗問，問之弗知，弗措也；有弗思，思之弗得，弗措也；有弗辨，辨之弗明，弗措也，有弗行，行之弗篤，弗措也。人一能之己百之，人十能之己千之。果能此道矣，雖愚必明，雖柔必強。」

"In all things success depends on previous preparation, and without such previous preparation there is sure to be failure. If what is to be spoken be previously determined, there will be no stumbling. If affairs be previously determined, there will be no difficulty with them. If one's actions have been previously determined, there will be no sorrow in connection with them. If principles of conduct have been previously determined, the practice of them will be inexhaustible. When those in inferior situations do not obtain the confidence of the sovereign, they cannot succeed in governing the people. There is a way to obtain the confidence of the sovereign;-if one is not trusted by his friends, he will not get the confidence of his sovereign. There is a way to being trusted by one's friends;-if one is not obedient to his parents, he will not be true to friends. There is a way to being obedient to one's parents;-if one, on turning his thoughts in upon himself, finds a want of sincerity, he will not be obedient to his parents. There is a way to the attainment of sincerity in one's self; -if a man do not understand what is good, he will not attain sincerity in himself. Sincerity is the way of Heaven. The attainment of sincerity is the way of men. He who possesses sincerity is he who, without an effort, hits what is right, and apprehends, without the exercise of thought;-he is the sage who naturally and easily embodies the right way. He who attains to sincerity is he who chooses what is good, and firmly holds it fast. To this attainment there are requisite the extensive study of what is good, accurate inquiry about it, careful reflection on it, the clear discrimination of it, and the earnest practice of it. The superior man, while there is anything he has not studied, or while in what he has studied there is anything he cannot understand, will not intermit his labor. While there is anything he has not inquired about, or anything in what he has inquired about which he does not know, he will not intermit his labor. While there is anything which he has not reflected on, or anything in what he has reflected on which he does not apprehend, he will not intermit his labor. While there is anything which he has not discriminated or his discrimination is not clear, he will not intermit his labor. If there be anything which he has not practiced, or his practice fails in earnestness, he will not intermit his labor. If another man succeed by one effort, he will use a hundred efforts. If another man succeed by ten efforts, he will use a thousand. Let a man proceed in this way, and, though dull, he will surely become intelligent; though weak, he will surely become strong."

自誠明，謂之性；自明誠，謂之教。誠則明矣，明則誠矣。唯天下至誠，為能盡其性；能盡其性，則能盡人之性；能盡人之性，則能盡物之性；能盡物之性，則可以贊天地之化育；可以贊天地之化育，則可以與天地參矣。

When we have intelligence resulting from sincerity, this condition is to be ascribed to nature; when we have sincerity resulting from intelligence, this condition is to be ascribed to instruction. But given the sincerity, and there shall be the intelligence; given the intelligence, and there shall be the sincerity. It is only he who is possessed of the most complete sincerity that can exist under heaven, who can give its full development to his nature. Able to give its full development to his own nature, he can do the same to the nature of other men. Able to give its full development to the nature of other men, he can give their full development to the natures of animals and things. Able to give their full development to the natures of creatures and things, he can assist the transforming and nourishing powers of Heaven and Earth. Able to assist the transforming and nourishing powers of Heaven and Earth, he may with Heaven and Earth form a ternion.

其次致曲。曲能有誠，誠則形，形則著，著則明，明則動，動則變，變則化。唯天下至誠為能化。

Next to the above is he who cultivates to the utmost the shoots of goodness in him. From those he can attain to the possession of sincerity. This sincerity becomes apparent. From being apparent, it becomes manifest. From being manifest, it becomes brilliant. Brilliant, it affects others. Affecting others, they are changed by it. Changed by it, they are transformed. It is only he who is possessed of the most complete sincerity that can exist under heaven, who can transform.

至誠之道，可以前知。國家將興，必有禎祥；國家將亡，必有妖孽。見乎蓍龜，動乎四體。禍福將至：善，必先知之；不善，必先知之。故至誠如神。

It is characteristic of the most entire sincerity to be able to foreknow. When a nation or family is about to flourish, there are sure to be happy omens; and when it is about to perish, there are sure to be unlucky omens. Such events are seen in the milfoil and tortoise, and affect the movements of the four limbs. When calamity or happiness is about to come, the good shall certainly be foreknown by him, and the evil also. Therefore the individual possessed of the most complete sincerity is like a spirit.

誠者自成也，而道自道也。誠者物之終始，不誠無物。是故君子誠之為貴。誠者非自成己而已也，所以成物也。成己，仁也；成物，知也。性之德也，合外內之道也，故時措之宜也。故至誠無息。不息則久，久則徵，徵則悠遠，悠遠則博厚，博厚則高明。博厚，所以載物也；高明，所以覆物也；悠久，所以成物也。博厚配地，高明配天，悠久無疆。如此者，不見而章，不動而變，無為而成。

Sincerity is that whereby self-completion is effected, and its way is that by which man must direct himself. Sincerity is the end and beginning of things; without sincerity there would be nothing. On this account, the superior man regards the attainment of sincerity as the most excellent thing. The possessor of sincerity does not merely accomplish the self-completion of himself. With this quality he completes other men and things also. The completing himself shows his perfect virtue. The completing other men and things shows his knowledge. But these are virtues belonging to the nature, and this is the way by which a union is effected of the external and internal. Therefore, whenever he-the entirely sincere man-employs them,-that is, these virtues, their action will be right. Hence to entire sincerity there belongs ceaselessness. Not ceasing, it continues long. Continuing long, it evidences itself. Evidencing itself, it reaches far. Reaching far, it becomes large and substantial. Large and substantial, it becomes high and brilliant. Large and substantial;-this is how it contains all things. High and brilliant;-this is how it overspreads all things. Reaching far and continuing long;-this is how it perfects all things. So large and substantial, the individual possessing it is the co-equal of Earth. So high and brilliant, it makes him the co-equal of Heaven. So far-reaching and long-continuing, it makes him infinite. Such being its nature, without any display, it becomes manifested; without any movement, it produces changes; and without any effort, it accomplishes its ends.

天地之道，可壹言而盡也。其為物不貳，則其生物不測。天地之道，博也厚也，高也明也，悠也久也。今夫天，斯昭昭之多，及其無窮也，日月星辰系焉，萬物覆焉。今夫地，一撮土之多，及其廣厚，載華岳而不重，振河海而不泄，萬物載焉。今夫山，一拳石之多，及其廣大，草木生之，禽獸居之，寶藏興焉。今夫水，一勺之多，及其不測，黿鼉、蛟龍、魚鱉生焉，貨財殖焉。《詩》云：「維天之命，於穆不已！」蓋曰天之所以為天也。「於乎不顯！文王之德之純！」蓋曰文王之所以為文也，純亦不已。

The way of Heaven and Earth may be completely declared in one sentence. They are without any doubleness, and so they produce things in a manner that is unfathomable. The way of Heaven and Earth is large and substantial, high and brilliant, far-reaching and long-enduring. The Heaven now before us is only this bright shining spot; but when viewed in its inexhaustible extent, the sun, moon, stars, and constellations of the zodiac, are suspended in it, and all things are overspread by it. The earth before us is but a handful of soil; but when regarded in its breadth and thickness, it sustains mountains like the Hwa and the Yo, without feeling their weight, and contains the rivers and seas, without their leaking away. The mountain now before us appears only a stone; but when contemplated in all the vastness of its size, we see how the grass and trees are produced on it, and birds and beasts dwell on it, and precious things which men treasure up are found on it. The water now before us appears but a ladleful; yet extending our view to its unfathomable depths, the largest tortoises, iguanas, iguanodons, dragons, fishes, and turtles, are produced in it, articles of value and sources of wealth abound in it. It is said in the Book of Poetry, "The ordinances of Heaven, how profound are they and unceasing!" The meaning is, that it is thus that Heaven is Heaven. And again, "How illustrious was it, the singleness of the virtue of King Wen!" indicating that it was thus that King Wen was what he was. Singleness likewise is unceasing.

大哉，聖人之道！洋洋乎發育萬物，峻極于天。優優大哉！禮儀三百，威儀三千，待其人然後行。故曰：苟不至德，至道不凝焉。故君子尊德性而道問學，致廣大而盡精微，極高明而中庸。溫故而知新，敦厚以崇禮。是故居上不驕，為下不倍；國有道，其言足以興，國無道，其默足以容。《詩》曰：「既明且哲，以保其身。」其此之謂與！

How great is the path proper to the Sage! Like overflowing water, it sends forth and nourishes all things, and rises up to the height of heaven. All-complete is its greatness! It embraces the three hundred rules of ceremony, and the three thousand rules of demeanor. It waits for the proper man, and then it is trodden. Hence it is said, "Only by perfect virtue can the perfect path, in all its courses, be made a fact." Therefore, the superior man honors his virtuous nature, and maintains constant inquiry and study, seeking to carry it out to its breadth and greatness, so as to omit none of the more exquisite and minute points which it embraces, and to raise it to its greatest height and brilliancy, so as to pursue the course of the Mean. He cherishes his old knowledge, and is continually acquiring new. He exerts an honest, generous earnestness, in the esteem and practice of all propriety. Thus, when occupying a high situation he is not proud, and in a low situation he is not insubordinate. When the kingdom is well governed, he is sure by his words to rise; and when it is ill governed, he is sure by his silence to command forbearance to himself. Is not this what we find in the Book of Poetry,-"Intelligent is he and prudent, and so preserves his person?"

子曰：「愚而好自用，賤而好自專，生乎今之世，反古之道。如此者，災及其身者也。」非天子，不議禮，不制度，不考文。今天下車同軌，書同文，行同倫。雖有其位，苟無其德，不敢作禮樂焉；雖有其德，苟無其位，亦不敢作禮樂焉。

The Master said, Let a man who is ignorant be fond of using his own judgment; let a man without rank be fond of assuming a directing power to himself; let a man who is living in the present age go back to the ways of antiquity;-on the persons of all who act thus calamities will be sure to come. To no one but the Son of Heaven does it belong to order ceremonies, to fix the measures, and to determine the written characters. Now over the kingdom, carriages have all wheels, of-the-same size; all writing is with the same characters; and for conduct there are the same rules. One may occupy the throne, but if he have not the proper virtue, he may not dare to make ceremonies or music. One may have the virtue, but if he do not occupy the throne, he may not presume to make ceremonies or music.

子曰：「吾說夏禮，杞不足徵也。吾學殷禮，有宋存焉；吾學周禮，今用之，吾從周。」王天下有三重焉，其寡過矣乎！上焉者雖善無徵，無徵不信，不信民弗從；下焉者雖善不尊，不尊不信，不信民弗從。故君子之道本諸身，徵諸庶民，考諸三王而不繆，建諸天地而不悖，質諸鬼神而無疑，百世以俟聖人而不惑。質諸鬼神而無疑，知天也；百世以俟聖人而不惑，知人也。是故君子動而世為天下道，行而世為天下法，言而世為天下則。遠之則有望，近之則不厭。《詩》曰：「在彼無惡，在此無射；庶幾夙夜，以永終譽！」君子未有不如此而蚤有譽於天下者也。

The Master said, "I may describe the ceremonies of the Xia dynasty, but Qi cannot sufficiently attest my words. I have learned the ceremonies of the Yin dynasty, and in Song they still continue. I have learned the ceremonies of Zhou, which are now used, and I follow Zhou." He who attains to the sovereignty of the kingdom, having those three important things, shall be able to effect that there shall be few errors under his government. However excellent may have been the regulations of those of former times, they cannot be attested. Not being attested, they cannot command credence, and not being credited, the people would not follow them. However excellent might be the regulations made by one in an inferior situation, he is not in a position to be honored. Unhonored, he cannot command credence, and not being credited, the people would not follow his rules. Therefore the institutions of the Ruler are rooted in his own character and conduct, and sufficient attestation of them is given by the masses of the people. He examines them by comparison with those of the three kings, and finds them without mistake. He sets them up before Heaven and Earth, and finds nothing in them contrary to their mode of operation. He presents himself with them before spiritual beings, and no doubts about them arise. He is prepared to wait for the rise of a sage a hundred ages after, and has no misgivings. His presenting himself with his institutions before spiritual beings, without any doubts arising about them, shows that he knows Heaven. His being prepared, without any misgivings, to wait for the rise of a sage a hundred ages after, shows that he knows men. Such being the case, the movements of such a ruler, illustrating his institutions, constitute an example to the world for ages. His acts are for ages a law to the kingdom. His words are for ages a lesson to the kingdom. Those who are far from him look longingly for him; and those who are near him are never wearied with him. It is said in the Book of Poetry,-"Not disliked there, not tired of here, from day to day and night tonight, will they perpetuate their praise." Never has there been a ruler, who did not realize this description, that obtained an early renown throughout the kingdom.

仲尼祖述堯、舜，憲章文、武；上律天時，下襲水土。辟如天地之無不持載，無不覆幬，辟如四時之錯行，如日月之代明。萬物并育而不相害，道并行而不相悖，小德川流，大德敦化，此天地之所以為大也。

Zhong-ni handed down the doctrines of Yao and Shun, as if they had been his ancestors, and elegantly displayed the regulations of Wen and Wu taking them as his model. Above, he harmonized with the times of Heaven, and below, he was conformed to the water and land. He may be compared to Heaven and Earth in their supporting and containing, their overshadowing and curtaining, all things. He may be compared to the four seasons in their alternating progress, and to the sun and moon in their successive shining. All things are nourished together without their injuring one another. The courses of the seasons, and of the sun and moon, are pursued without any collision among them. The smaller energies are like river currents; the greater energies are seen in mighty transformations. It is this which makes heaven and earth so great.

唯天下至聖，為能聰明睿知，足以有臨也；寬裕溫柔，足以有容也；發強剛毅，足以有執也；齊莊中正，足以有敬也；文理密察，足以有別也。溥博淵泉，而時出之。溥博如天，淵泉如淵。見而民莫不敬，言而民莫不信，行而民莫不說。是以聲名洋溢乎中國，施及蠻貊；舟車所至，人力所通，天之所覆，地之所載，日月所照，霜露所隊；凡有血氣者，莫不尊親，故曰配天。

It is only he, possessed of all sagely qualities that can exist under heaven, who shows himself quick in apprehension, clear in discernment, of far-reaching intelligence, and all-embracing knowledge, fitted to exercise rule; magnanimous, generous, benign, and mild, fitted to exercise forbearance; impulsive, energetic, firm, and enduring, fitted to maintain a firm hold; self-adjusted, grave, never swerving from the Mean, and correct, fitted to command reverence; accomplished, distinctive, concentrative, and searching, fitted to exercise discrimination. All-embracing is he and vast, deep and active as a fountain, sending forth in their due season his virtues. All-embracing and vast, he is like Heaven. Deep and active as a fountain, he is like the abyss. He is seen, and the people all reverence him; he speaks, and the people all believe him; he acts, and the people all are pleased with him. Therefore his fame overspreads the Middle Kingdom, and extends to all barbarous tribes. Wherever ships and carriages reach; wherever the strength of man penetrates; wherever the heavens overshadow and the earth sustains; wherever the sun and moon shine; wherever frosts and dews fall:-all who have blood and breath unfeignedly honor and love him. Hence it is said, "He is the equal of Heaven."

唯天下至誠，為能經綸天下之大經，立天下之大本，知天地之化育。夫焉有所倚？肫肫其仁！淵淵其淵！浩浩其天！苟不固聰明聖知達天德者，其孰能知之？

It is only the individual possessed of the most entire sincerity that can exist under Heaven, who can adjust the great invariable relations of mankind, establish the great fundamental virtues of humanity, and know the transforming and nurturing operations of Heaven and Earth;-shall this individual have any being or anything beyond himself on which he depends? Call him man in his ideal, how earnest is he! Call him an abyss, how deep is he! Call him Heaven, how vast is he! Who can know him, but he who is indeed quick in apprehension, clear in discernment, of far-reaching intelligence, and all-embracing knowledge, possessing all Heavenly virtue?

《詩》曰：「衣錦尚絅」，惡其文之著也。故君子之道，闇然而日章；小人之道，的然而日亡。君子之道：淡而不厭，簡而文，溫而理，知遠之近，知風之自，知微之顯，可與入德矣。

It is said in the Book of Poetry, "Over her embroidered robe she puts a plain single garment," intimating a dislike to the display of the elegance of the former. Just so, it is the way of the superior man to prefer the concealment of his virtue, while it daily becomes more illustrious, and it is the way of the mean man to seek notoriety, while he daily goes more and more to ruin. It is characteristic of the superior man, appearing insipid, yet never to produce satiety; while showing a simple negligence, yet to have his accomplishments recognized; while seemingly plain, yet to be discriminating. He knows how what is distant lies in what is near. He knows where the wind proceeds from. He knows how what is minute becomes manifested. Such a one, we may be sure, will enter into virtue.

《詩》云：「潛雖伏矣，亦孔之昭！」故君子內省不疚，無惡於志。君子所不可及者，其唯人之所不見乎！

It is said in the Book of Poetry, "Although the fish sink and lie at the bottom, it is still quite clearly seen." Therefore the superior man examines his heart, that there may be nothing wrong there, and that he may have no cause for dissatisfaction with himself. That wherein the superior man cannot be equaled is simply this,-his work which other men cannot see.

《詩》云:「相在爾室,尚不愧于屋漏。」故君子不動而敬,不言而信。

It is said in the Book of Poetry, "Looked at in your apartment, be there free from shame as being exposed to the light of Heaven." Therefore, the superior man, even when he is not moving, has a feeling of reverence, and while he speaks not, he has the feeling of truthfulness.

《詩》曰：「奏假無言，時靡有爭。」是故君子不賞而民勸，不怒而民威於鈇鉞。

It is said in the Book of Poetry, "In silence is the offering presented, and the spirit approached to; there is not the slightest contention." Therefore the superior man does not use rewards, and the people are stimulated to virtue. He does not show anger, and the people are awed more than by hatchets and battle-axes.

《詩》曰：「不顯惟德！百辟其刑之。」是故君子篤恭而天下平。

It is said in the Book of Poetry, "What needs no display is virtue. All the princes imitate it." Therefore, the superior man being sincere and reverential, the whole world is conducted to a state of happy tranquility.

《詩》曰：「予懷明德，不大聲以色。」子曰：「聲色之於以化民，末也。」《詩》曰：「德輶如毛」，毛猶有倫；「上天之載，無聲無臭」，至矣！

It is said in the Book of Poetry, "I regard with pleasure your brilliant virtue, making no great display of itself in sounds and appearances." The Master said, "Among the appliances to transform the people, sound and appearances are but trivial influences. It is said in another ode, 'His Virtue is light as a hair.' Still, a hair will admit of comparison as to its size. 'The doings of the supreme Heaven have neither sound nor smell.' That is perfect virtue."

Copyright © 2019 by FV Éditions
ISBN 9791029907975
All rights reserved.

www.ingramcontent.com/pod-product-compliance
Lightning Source LLC
LaVergne TN
LVHW091545070526
838199LV00002B/221